From Best-Selling Author

SHARLA J FROST

POWER AT THE TABLE^2

The Lawyer's Guide to Gaining
Clients and Control

Quantity sales and special discounts are available for bulk purchases by corporations, associations and others. For details, please reach out to CSI Publishing, listed above.

Orders by U.S. trade bookstores and wholesalers,

Email: ken@clientsi.com

The author can be reached through Ken Walls.

Manufactured and printed in the United States of America, distributed globally by CSI Publishing - www.clientsi.com

CSI Publishing

Dallas, Texas

Library of Congress Control number: 2025918027

ISBN: 978-1-963986-16-7 Paperback

ISBN: 978-1-963986-15-0 Hardback

ISBN: 978-1-963986-17-4 eBook

ALSO BY SHARLA J FROST

Business Series

Power At The Table: The Woman Lawyer's Guide to Gaining Clients and Control

Children's Series

Frogville: Quest of A Frog

Frogville: Quest of A Princess

Frogville: Quest For A Queen

Frogville: Quest for a Sword

Frogville: Quest for a King

Frogville: Quest for The Magic Beans,

Frogville: Quest for the Lost Boys (coming in October 2025)

Chapter Contributions

A Cup of Cappuccino for the Entrepreneur's Spirit, Volume 1 (multiple authors) 2009,

Speak Your Way To Success (multiple authors) 2020,

RockStar Entrepreneurs: Expert Tips, Valuable Insights, and Inspiring Stories from Extraordinary Business Leaders (multiple authors) 2024,

The Abundant Life, Top Thought-Leaders Share Their Secrets for Living an Extraordinary Life

ENDORSEMENTS

"Sharla Frost will thoughtlessly throw on the necessary overalls, gloves and boots and delve into the farm life and community where she grew up and still calls home. Her commitment to the betterment and legacy of her family home and town has led her to ventures, many of which most of us have never even contemplated. And she does so with determination and joy.

She can equally as gracefully throw on a beautiful suit and a pair of heels, strut right into any courtroom in the country and master the room with the same determination and joy.

Beyond her clear brilliance and intellect, this is what sets Sharla apart; her genius with perspectives. She has an exceptional ability to put herself inside the minds of all of us- no matter all the qualifiers, discriminators, and lines of separation we might claim exist. She doesn't just see other points of view. She wraps her head around them and truly understands them. This is why she's the master. The jurors know. She's not putting on a show of smooth but insincere lawyering. She knows and understands their hearts and minds, and she speaks to them directly.

Any trial attorney (or aspiring attorney) who truly wants to learn...Power at the Table is your trove of the best advice, wisdom and guidance."

> - Ellis Iverson, Law office of Ellis Iverson, Houston, family advocate, former associate attorney of Sharla's and long time mentee

One of our profession's most experienced and engaging speakers, litigators, and business development professionals, Sharla brings her expansive toolkit to her readers and inspires us all who want to build and expand their practice. Her insightful and motivational book, Power at the Table, is simply a "must read" for all lawyers interested in not only building their skill set, client base, and practice, but also in finding one's true talents and how to mobilize them for career success. Good luck Sharla! You're amazing!

- Edward P. Abbot, Partner, Eckert Seamans, New York City

Sharla has been a boss, mentor and later a colleague to me for over 20 years. I have benefited from her knowledge and experience both professionally and personally over that time. Sharla is well known throughout the legal community nationally as a formidable advocate for her clients, and is respected on both sides of the aisle for her professionalism and expertise. Any lawyer who is looking to increase their business and learn how to serve clients in a way that will not only keep them sending work, but also have them recommending you to others, would be well served to learn from her experience.

- Chip Adams, Partner, Gordon Rees Scully Mansukhani, Houston

POWER AT THE TABLE

The Lawyer's Guide to Gaining Clients and Control

Table of Contents

INTRODUCTION

HE HAD CLIENTS-I HAD CREDIT

There's a myth in the legal profession that if you just do great work, the rest will take care of itself. That skill and diligence alone will lead to recognition, opportunities, and long-term success. That work will flow like manna from heaven, and you will need only to be loyal and diligent to succeed. But anyone who's spent more than a few years in practice knows better. My personal experience should provide an example.

I knew something was up when my boss walked into the office at 2:00 in the afternoon and asked, "Wanna go have a beer?" It turned out he and I were both looking for new jobs. He was looking because he and his partners no longer shared a common vision; I was looking because his partners and I had never shared a common vision. Two minutes into the meeting over beer, he asked if I would leave the law firm to go with him to start a new one. Then, he offered to make me an equal partner. I was 33 years old, had no clients of my own, had no business training, and had no background in running a business—my own or someone else's. So, I, of course, immediately said, "Yes."

I consulted with my dad's elderly lawyer friend in Hugo, Oklahoma, who laughed until the day he died about telling me there was nothing he knew less about than starting a law firm in Houston! However, he gave me great advice: "You're young, and you don't have much money. If it doesn't work out, you won't have lost much, and you can find another job." He was right on both counts. I closed my eyes and jumped off the precipice. I had become an entrepreneur without really planning to. Without realizing it, I had also become a business generator.

We were lucky to have his clients and my credit card to start, but that wasn't going to sustain us for long. We needed more clients and more work if we were going to be successful. So began my journey into the world of client development–something law school did not warn me about or train me for.

Whether you're at a global law firm or a small-town solo practice, the ability to attract and retain clients isn't just a "nice to have"—it's a career cornerstone. Yet, most lawyers receive little to no training in how to build a book of business. We're taught how to think like a lawyer, not how to thrive as one.

That's where this book comes in. The pages that follow are thoughts and experiences gained from almost 20 years of managing our boutique law firm, later managing the regional office of a mega-firm, and then later still serving as a partner in a mid-sized firm. I am convinced that lawyers need more encouragement, more training, and more support in their individual business development efforts. At my boutique firm, I gladly claimed the title "Marketing Nag," because someone had to do it. I will not nag you in these pages, but I do hope to share some observations that make it possible for you to manage your own legal life, without having someone else in charge.

Power at the Table is a guide for lawyers who want to take ownership of their practice, their income, and their influence. Originally written to empower women attorneys in private practice, it has now been revised to speak to all lawyers—across practice areas, backgrounds, and stages of career—who want more than just a seat in the room. They want power at the table.

Inside, you'll find practical strategies, candid stories, and actionable worksheets designed to help you:

- Define your career vision and personal brand
- Identify your ideal clients and how to reach them
- Leverage your strengths for authentic marketing
- Cultivate a network that supports and sustains your growth

- Convert contacts into clients—and manage those relationships for the long term

Reputation matters. Relationships matter. And above all, business development matters.

You don't have to be the most outgoing person in the room. You don't have to have the biggest résumé or the loudest voice. What you do need is clarity, consistency, and the willingness to take initiative.

This book will show you how to do just that.

No matter where you start, you have the power to build the career you want. Let's begin.

KEY SUCCESS FACTORS:

Perseverance, Determination, Work Ethic, and Focus

RECOMMENDED READING:

Freakonomics by Steven D. Levitt;

The Tipping Point by Malcolm Gladwell

PART I

KNOW WHAT YOU WANT

"You can't build a reputation on what you are going to do."

– Henry Ford

CHAPTER 1

WHO DO YOU WANT TO BE?

Vision. Or, as it's sometimes called in Texan political circles, "that vision thingy." Whatever you call it, vision separates long-term success from short-term excitement.

You need a vision for your legal career—who you want to be as a lawyer and what role you want to play within your firm, your practice, or the broader legal profession. Somewhere deep inside, you probably already know whether you're a trial lawyer, a strategic counselor, a tax technician, or an appellate tactician. You likely have a sense of whether you want to lead a firm or thrive in a focused practice area, whether you prefer flying solo or collaborating in a bustling team. No matter the role that calls to you, you must first name it—and then build the roadmap to reach it.

Some readers may already have defined their area of practice and determined whether they want to contribute to law firm leadership. Others may still be discovering their professional identity. In either case, it is easy for personal vision to be eclipsed by billable deadlines and the urgency of client service. That's why intentionality matters.

Take time to assess your goals, your plan, and your dream for your career. Then evaluate your current position in relation to that vision. When you identify that gap, you can chart a path. Without that map, it's easy to spend your days reacting to life instead of building a practice.

Strategic planning should become a daily discipline—not just for business development, but for your own career. Block time each week to work on your career the way you work on a case: systematically, with deadlines, and with purpose.

One powerful way to start is to understand your value within your current organization. Look at the financial data that management uses to evaluate your contributions. Do you know how much you cost the firm? What percentage of the money you bring in goes toward your compensation and benefits? How does your realization rate compare with your peers?

You need to perform an objective analysis concerning your own position relative to the profession and your firm. Step one of the process: understand your financial status within the firm. Understand the value, or profit margin of the dollars you generate, and then compare that profit number to the dollars you take out in terms of benefits and salary.

In other words, what do you cost the firm? What percent of recovered dollars constitutes your compensation? How does your financial production compare your cost to the firm, and what is the delta—or difference— between the two? Firm management tracks that data.

Most firms have very sophisticated software to permit the decision makers to evaluate the financial value of every lawyer and billable staff member. Even small firms track the value of work in progress (WIP), accounts receivable, and the realization rate, or recovery rate, for each lawyer. You should know that information for yourself and track it, as well. See the Power Projection Worksheet at the end of this chapter for a sample worksheet to assist you in tracking those numbers.

This isn't about vanity. It's about clarity. Law firms are businesses, and most firms—big and small—track the profitability of each lawyer. If they are doing the math, you should be, too.

Once you have a thorough understanding of your current financial position within the law firm, you will be able to analyze how to improve your financial situation and your status within the firm. To increase your power in the organization, you need to expand the profit margin of the work that you originate and control within the firm. The way to improve those statistics both for yourself and the firm is to establish your own area of expertise and expand your own book of business. There are several separate components to that process.

After satisfying yourself of the need to improve your financial lot in life, step one is to envision what you want your case load to include, as well as what you want your firm role to be. If you are a senior level lawyer, partner or not, that should include which management committees you want to join. The next step is to develop a specific plan to turn your vision into reality. In the chapters that follow, we will explore the process of expanding your personal book of business through establishing your personal and professional brand, developing your network of contacts and potential clients, and then, converting those branding and networking activities into tangible, billable work that provides you the ability to control client relationships. Understanding that process will, ultimately, provide you with greater financial power within the firm and more power within the profession.

Take the time to run the numbers. Use the worksheet at the end of this chapter to estimate your production, your realization, and your compensation delta. That data gives you a benchmark from which to grow.

Once you have the baseline, ask yourself: What do I want my practice to look like in three years? In five years? What kind of cases or transactions do I want to handle? What clients do I want to serve? What committees do I want to sit on? Who do I want calling me for advice?

And here's the key: Don't just imagine it. Write it down. Be specific. Then make a plan to get there.

In the chapters that follow, we'll cover how to build a reputation in your chosen specialty, how to expand your professional network, and how to turn that network into a thriving book of business. Because whether you're a junior associate, a solo practitioner, or a name partner, the lawyer who controls the client relationship controls his future.

You don't need to wait for someone else to open a door. You can build the room—and sit at the head of the table. That's the power you want.

KEY SUCCESS FACTORS:

Persistence, Self-awareness, Goal-setting.

ADDITIONAL READING:

https://www.alanet.org/legal-management/2024/march/columns/the-3-fs-of-client-development-for-law-firms

https://www.smokeball.com/blog/law-firm-growth-and-challenges-in-2024-a-global-survey-marketing-technology

Worksheet: Power Projections

1. Production Goals:

Goals for Year	Number	Description
Billable Hours		
Marketing Hours		
Administrative Hours		
(Firm Management)		
Community Service Hours		
Vacation Hours		

2. Financial Goals

Current Statistics	Dollar Value
Current Billing Rates	
Work in Progress Value	
Realization Rate	
Originating Attorney Credit	
Supervising Attorney Credit	
Working Attorney Credit	
Current Compensation Package (Salary or draw, plus benefits)	
Compensation Goal	

CHAPTER 2

DEVELOP EXPERTISE

Every solid marketing strategy begins with expertise. You have to know what you're selling before you ask anyone else to buy it. Clients today are discerning. Whether they are individuals, corporations, or public entities, most view legal services as interchangeable unless given a reason not to. Expertise is how you distinguish yourself.

Early in your legal career, developing expertise means learning your craft: how to respond to client needs, draft strategically, and deliver under pressure. You begin to discover which types of work interest you and which don't. As you build your practice, that interest should evolve into specialization. Follow legal developments in your chosen area. Study not only the law, but also the industry trends, client concerns, and emerging risks. This is how you transition from capable technician to trusted advisor.

If you are a new associate, you will, undoubtedly, still be getting your sea legs under you, trying to figure out how to do your work, bill your time, and manage the expectations of your bosses. At that stage, you need to learn the practice of law, which you will quickly discover is different from the legal principles you learned in law school. Practicing law involves the day-to-day business of handling your clients' needs. You will learn to answer the questions raised by their business difficulties, write the motions that advance their positions, and negotiate the resolutions for their disputes. You will also learn which substantive areas interest you and which do not.

Continue to study those areas that interest you. Keep up with the legal developments, whether they are court decisions or legislative changes. Follow the business and popular press on areas of the law where you want to focus your practice. In the early stages of your legal career, you are unlikely to have decision-making power over the substantive assignments you get. Remember, associates are typically considered to be fungible. Make it your mission to become the go-to associate in a substantive area that interests you, then become your firm's expert on that topic.

If you're more senior, your substantive area is likely well-established. You've put in the time, earned credibility, and can be trusted to get the job done. But business development requires more than capability—it demands clarity. Can you articulate what sets your services apart? Why should a client pick you instead of the hundreds of other competent lawyers out there?

Define what you do well and be able to express it succinctly. Then ensure your brand—the articles you write, the CLEs you teach, and the referrals you receive—aligns with that expertise.

I once had a colleague who pivoted from commercial litigation to employment law because she realized she wanted a change. She approached it with what I called Stalin's Five-Year Plan (minus the tyranny): she mapped out a strategic development path. First, she immersed herself in seminars and readings. Then she wrote articles and built thought leadership. Finally, she started speaking at conferences and alerting clients that she was expanding her practice. Within five years, she had become her firm's go-to employment lawyer with a portfolio of loyal clients.

To apply that approach yourself, you first need to prepare a short-term, mid-term, and long-term personal-development plan. The five-year plan is your long-term plan. Spend some time objectively thinking about what you would like your practice to look like in year five. Then, work backwards to establish the benchmarks to take you to that outcome. Think of it as a case management order for your career. The intermediate steps on that CMO constitute the benchmarks for your plan progress.

That strategy isn't just for people making practice area or lateral moves. Even if you're staying within your firm, you should have a short-, mid-, and long-term development plan. Think of it as a case management order for your career.

Set clear benchmarks:

- What do you want to be known for?
- Which industries or client types should associate your name with their issues?
- What publications and conferences align with your goals?

Now post that plan somewhere you'll see it every day. Not digitally, buried in a folder—visibly present in your workspace. Unless you have focus, you will find the five-year plan at the bottom of the pile during year six, and it will have been nothing more than a creative writing exercise.

Choose three immediate steps. Register for a key industry seminar. Pitch a CLE topic to your local bar association. Draft the outline of a white paper for publication. Be creative and find a logical opportunity to showcase your abilities and your interests.

These steps don't need to be massive. They just need to be real. Every plan should be different. It's personal. No one size fits all. So this is not an exercise someone else can do for you.

Expertise isn't a label—it's an investment. And once you've built it, you can leverage it to grow your book of business, shape your career, and define your professional narrative. Remember: clients hire lawyers, not résumés.

Does this not sound like business development? Perhaps not to some of you, but, yes, it is. You have to have something to market before you can become a marketing resource.

KEYWORDS:

Ambition, Foresight, Planning

ADDITIONAL READING:

"Your Individual Attorney Marketing Plan" John Remsen, http://www.theremsengroup.com/articles-full/2015/9/28/ your-individual-attorney marketing-plan

https://www.lawyer-monthly.com/2025/04/legal-marketing-in-2025-strategies-for-success-in-a-transforming-industry/

Worksheet: Expertise Mapping

Take a few minutes to sketch your expertise path:

1. Target Area

What practice area or subject do you want to be known for? Describe in 30 words or less.

_____

_____

2. Action Timeline

What three steps will you take in the next 90 days?

A. _____

B. _____

C. _____

3. Educational Plan

What articles, CLEs, or seminars should you attend or create in the next 12 months?

_____

_____

4. Visibility Strategy

Where can you publish or present to build authority in the next 24 months?

_____

_____

5. What is your five year plan? Describe in 30 words or less.

_____

_____

CHAPTER 3

MAXIMIZE YOUR BRAND

Do you recognize names like David Boies? Neal Katyal? Judge Judy? Sunny Hostin?

Why do those names stand out? Is it their courtroom prowess—or market saturation of names?

In truth, it's often the latter. Each of these lawyers has had a successful legal career, but they became widely known because they took control of their public presence. They became brands.

Many lawyers are uncomfortable with the idea of "selling" themselves. Some see it as boastful or inauthentic. Others simply don't know where to start. But here's the truth: if you don't define your professional identity, someone else will do it for you—or worse, no one will do it at all.

Branding isn't about self-promotion. It's about clarity and consistency. It's about ensuring your name is associated with the problems you solve and the value you deliver. You don't have to be on television. You don't need a podcast or a book deal (though those things don't hurt). You simply need to be recognizable to the people who matter most to your career.

What does that mean? Good options include writing articles on the issues you want to be known for. Speaking at events that attract the clients you want to serve. Being visible in the organizations that influence your industry or practice area.

Think of your professional brand as a magnet. When you're known for something specific, work starts coming to you. That's when the real power begins—when you attract work rather than chase it.

Take my own experience. For years, "Jim and Sharla" was a recognizable phrase in tort litigation circles. Whether they were clients, experts, or adversaries, people knew who we were. That reputation wasn't accidental. We worked hard to deliver excellent legal results, of course—but we also made sure to write, to speak, and to show up.

I had been trying cases for more than a decade when I was asked to present at a national asbestos defense seminar. I had the dreaded 8:00 a.m. Friday time slot—post-cocktail-party, pre-golf-tournament. The organizers expected a light turnout. Then the rain came, and the golf game was canceled. Suddenly, I had a packed house of 1,500 lawyers. Oh, and I happened to be wearing a hot pink jacket, which I had carefully chosen for the occasion. (Unbeknownst to me, three massive, football field sized screens behind me showed only me and not my carefully constructed PowerPoint presentation, which had crashed without anyone alerting me).

I had their attention. And I made the most of it. I had the opportunity to educate the audience about jury selection—a skill I was particularly known for.

To this day, lawyers I've never personally met come up and tell me they remember that presentation—and the pink jacket. That's the power of personal branding: you become memorable for the right reasons.

To start building your brand, you must have consistency. Your email signature, your website bio, your curriculum vitae, your speaking materials—they should all reflect the same voice and value proposition. You need visibility. Don't just belong to organizations—be active. Take a leadership role. Show up with purpose. And most importantly, you must have substance. Everything you share—articles, posts, talks—should reinforce your expertise. Quality matters.

Tom Peters, the well-known management guru, published on the concept of branding a couple decades ago. His theory is that everything about you should be immediately identifiable, from your publications to your forms. Your pre-printed firm materials probably have that approach. The firm logo on your business card is the same as the logo on your website and your email signature line. If yours looks different, you should change it. Is the difference subtle? Probably, but having a seamless presence is part of the development of your brand.

In similar fashion, your professional marketing correspondence should have the same feel, regardless of the target audience. Consider the tone of the letter or the note you write. The persona you project constitutes the heart of your personal brand. Make sure it conveys the message you want to send. Sloppy or inconsistent doesn't inspire confidence in the recipient. You want that recipient to become a contact and then a client. Don't give them an easy reason to reject you.

We live in a world where everyone wants to see the length of your curriculum vitae, the coveted legal CV. When meeting with a potential client, you want something that reflects the substantive strength that forms the foundation of your brand. You need a written package to demonstrate that you can solve whatever problem the client faces. As part of your branding activities, maintain an updated CV. Keep a list of the articles you write. Keep a list of the speeches you give. Keep a list of the organizations you join. If you're a trial lawyer, keep a list of the trials you handled, including the location and the names of the parties and the judge.

Branding doesn't happen by accident. It happens by design. You are your own best asset. Treat your name like it matters—because it does.

KEYWORDS:

Name recognition, Publicity, Branding

ADDITIONAL READING:

The Brand You 50: Fifty Ways to Transform Yourself from an 'Employee' into a Brand That Shouts Distinction, Commitment, and Passion! by Tom Peters, (Alfred A. Knopf Inc., 1999) Building a Story Brand 2.0: Clarify Your Message So Customers Will Listen by Donald Miller (Harper Collins, 2025)

Branding Worksheet

1. Personal Brand Words
List three words you want people to associate with you:

_____

2. Current Visibility Check
Do your online bio, LinkedIn, and any other social media and materials reflect three words you want people to associate with you? ☐ Yes ☐ No

If no, when and how will you fix them?

_____

_____

3. Opportunities for Visibility
Identify three places where you have name recognition (community organizations, Bar organizations, Bar or community committees, church, school groups, etc.):

_____

_____

Identify three other organizations where you could raise your profile:

_____

_____

Identify three organizations where you have (or could have) a leadership role

_____

_____

Identify three publications where you could publish an article:

_____

_____

PART II

KNOW WHO YOU WANT

"Know yourself to improve yourself."

-Auguste Comte

CHAPTER 4

IMAGINE YOUR PERFECT CLIENT

Once you've identified your preferred area of legal practice and established your brand pillars, it's time to think about the client side of the equation. Just as some cases fit your skills and temperament better than others, some clients are a better match for your practice than others.

Who is your perfect or dream client?

That's not a rhetorical question. Get specific. Think about the cases or matters you've enjoyed most. Who were you working with? What kind of issues were you solving? What made the collaboration successful—substantively and financially?

Your dream client should be identifiable not just by industry or matter type, but by behavior, communication style, and expectations. You're not just looking for someone who can hire you—you're looking for a client with whom you can build a sustainable, respectful, and mutually beneficial relationship.[1]

Your dream client should also be identifiable and describable from both a substantive and a logistics standpoint. The billable rate and the quality of work should both go into your calculation of the right client, or type of client, for you to target. Your value

---

[1] *This and the following discussion assume that the reader is familiar with the ABA Model Rules of Professional Conduct, as well as any applicable state regulations concerning attorney-client relationships. A discussion of those issues is beyond the scope of this book. However, I recommend that you consider the ethical boundaries of any business development program you or your firm implement. Consult your in-house ethics counsel if you have any questions. If you do not have an in-house ethics counsel, call your State Bar Ethics Counsel and get their input on any questions you may have.*

within the profession includes professional satisfaction you get from doing the work, as well the financial return you receive for having done it. You need to think about the financial value of the work you are seeking when you describe your ideal client.

There are endless opportunities to be hired for work that either does not pay or does not pay well. Those are not the types of assignments you should target if your goal is to increase the value of your book of business. Your position of power within the firm depends, in significant part, on the size of the accounts receivables you control. For that reason, your evaluation of potential clients and work assignments must include a financial evaluation.

Think about these core considerations: Does the client engage in matters that fall within your area of expertise? Do they communicate clearly, provide timely feedback, and treat their legal counsel as a partner, not just a vendor? Can they pay your rate? Will the work be steady enough to justify the investment of your time and energy?

Too many lawyers fall into the trap of chasing every potential matter, regardless of fit. The excitement of being chosen can cloud your professional judgment. But here's the truth: not all business is good business.

When the fit is off—when expectations, values, or workflows don't align—it costs you more than it pays. Your practice thrives when your client portfolio aligns with your professional goals and your firm's strategic vision.

I've had the misfortune of taking on a client that wasn't the right match. The substance of the work was in my wheelhouse, but our preferred approaches couldn't have been more different. They wanted a lean, singular legal lead—"one riot, one Ranger," as the saying goes. I ran a team-based shop, built for complex, high-volume matters. We both suffered from unmet expectations and a lack of clear communication. The outcome wasn't failure—it was misalignment. And it could have been avoided if we had taken the time to talk, listen, and evaluate fit more honestly from the beginning.

It would be hard to say who was more excited when the assignment ended: me or the client. That experience caused me to evaluate potential clients more carefully when I was being offered work. Due-diligence on clients who are making new assignments, or changing existing assignments, can help both sides avoid a mismatch.

Learn from my experience. Be deliberate about the business you pursue.

When you identify the characteristics of the client or type of client you would like to have in your originating-attorney column, write them down. Make a checklist of the attributes you want in your client collection.

Your checklist of ideal client characteristics should consider some or all of the following attributes:

- Industry or sector
- Type of legal needs
- Size and complexity of matters
- Communication preferences
- Budget and billing compatibility
- Ethical and cultural alignment

Once you have refined your checklist, then put content to your vision. Create a list of actual companies, organizations, agencies, or individuals who fit that profile. Think of it as the professional equivalent of your Christmas wish list. Not a dream—an intention.

We'll build on this in the next chapter, where we begin the process of converting these ideal profiles into specific, actionable leads.

KEY SUCCESS FACTORS:

Insight; Planning; Honesty

ADDITIONAL READING:

"Choosing Clients: Why It's Important and How You Can Do It" James Nicolle, January 23, 2018 https://www.boost.co.nz/blog/2018/01/ choosing-clients

https://www.americanbar.org/groups/law_practice/resources/law-technology-today/2025/the-legal-industry-report-2025/

Worksheet: Client Profile Builder

Define your ideal client clearly and strategically:

Client Name	Contact Person	Contact email	Planned Action	Due Date	Next step
Widget Company, USA	William Robert Smith	billybobsmith@ widget.usa.scam	Send latest firm brochure	Next Friday	

CHAPTER 5

MAKE A LIST

After all that introspection in Chapter 4, you should have identified your dream client. You've thought through the industries, individuals, and types of matters that align with your expertise and vision. Now it's time to get specific.

Take a piece of paper and either a pen or pencil, and write down the names of six potential clients—actual people or organizations—you'd like to represent. Not "I'd like to work with a Fortune 100 company." Instead, "I'd like to work with ACME Corporation, and the person who makes decisions there is Sam Patel, General Counsel." There is something magic about putting pen to paper.

Post the list somewhere you'll see it every day, just like you did with the list of your career plans. Put it next to your monitor. Take a photo and save it as your phone's lock screen. This isn't just a professional exercise—it's a mindset tool. The act of writing it down helps clarify intention and drive action. The list itself serves as a reminder of your destination. Pair it with a photograph of the retirement cottage you intend to buy with the increased compensation you'll receive from work generated by those new clients. Let the list and the photograph invigorate your daily efforts.

The list should be an inspirational note, not an encyclopedia of every possible client you would want to work for, if you could. Narrow the list down to six. Six is a manageable number. More than that, and the task becomes vague and overwhelming. Fewer, and it lacks momentum. With six names, you can rotate your focus throughout the year, dedicating real time and attention to each.

For each potential client, ask yourself: Who is the decision-maker or hiring officer within the company? Do you already have a connection to that person? What's your first step toward making or strengthening the relationship? What problem do they have that you can help them solve?

The Internet overflows with lists of companies and compilations of categories of companies. There are a variety of commercially-available databases that include the names, titles, email addresses, and telephone numbers of the people who make the decisions within corporate legal departments. Some companies have specific hiring officers for all outside vendors, including lawyers. Your list should include the details you need to contact those decision makers, whether they are lawyers or not. You cannot expect to get hired if you have not done the necessary research to figure out who will make that decision.

Treat the search for the appropriate contact person like you would treat a discovery assignment in a lawsuit: the more detail you can find, the more likely you are to get your foot in the door—as we will discuss in more detail in chapter nine.

Treat this list like your personal business development docket. Just as you calendar deadlines and court appearances, you should calendar your outreach and engagement plans for each name on this list.

When my boutique firm and I were in the midst of a robust marketing program, we spent a significant amount of money on a cutting-edge database that was, at the time, provided by Westlaw. I used it to research companies that had significant product liability litigation, which was the type of work I wanted to do. I compiled an Excel spreadsheet of all the companies that had a litigation profile that seemed to meet our targeted characteristics and also had litigation needs we could meet. For those, I pulled their Dun & Bradstreet profile, their last three

10-K reports, and a list of litigation they had pending. After narrowing the list to those who had litigation in my geographic area, I used the database to identify the legal department or the business section officers who controlled the outside legal spending. I kept a list of the name, contact information, and planned activity that would be my next step to meeting that person, or if it was someone I had already met, what was the next interaction I had planned for that person. I used a calendar-reminder system to keep track of the actions taken and any necessary follow-up.

You can do something similar. Your "list" doesn't have to be complex. An Excel sheet works just fine. The point is to be deliberate. These names aren't just hopes. They are strategic targets.

Calendar. Calendar. Calendar. Follow-up. Repeat. If it's not on the calendar, your regularly-scheduled events, work tasks, and daily emergencies will consume all your time. Treat the tasks you set for your business development plan just like you treat a case deadline. Make them a priority. Remember, the earlier in the year you can get the new client in the door, the larger the account recovery for the year, and the more significant an effect those recoveries will have on your annual compensation.

Make sure you schedule a next step for each name on your list:

- Ask someone in your network for an introduction, if you need one.
- Send an article they might find useful.
- Invite them to a CLE or webinar.
- Reach out directly with a thoughtful, relevant message.

Then, calendar your follow-ups from those initial activities. That's right—put reminders on your phone or in your case management system. Treat each of these actions as seriously as you would a court deadline. Because the deadline you miss on business development may be the one that costs you growth you didn't even know you were capable of.

KEYWORDS:

Tenacity; Resolve

ADDITIONAL READING:

"Find Your Customers With A Target Market Analysis" Mike Kappel,

https://www.forbes.com/sites/mikekappel/2017/01/09/find-your customers-with-a-target-market-analysis/#6c69204d-6bab

https://www.thomsonreuters.com/en-us/posts/legal/insights-in-action-addressing-clients-priorities/

Worksheet: Target Client Worksheet

Company	Contact	Phone Number	Email	Planned Action

CHAPTER 6

EXPAND YOUR CIRCLE

When it comes to business development, your easiest starting points are often right in front of you: existing clients and your professional colleagues. For existing clients, you want to develop the reputation of doing the best, most reliable work of any lawyer they can use. That means doing a thorough job on any research or drafting; making sure that you meet or exceed all deadlines. As one of my former associates used to tell me, "The best marketing is to do great work."

Let's begin with existing clients. If you already have client relationships, ask yourself: Are you offering the full scope of your expertise? Are you seen as someone they can trust with more work? One of the most effective marketing strategies is also the simplest—do exceptional work. Meet deadlines, respond promptly, and deliver high-quality legal service. That level of diligence builds trust and opens doors.

If you're at a firm, dig a little deeper. Are there current clients your firm already serves that haven't yet been exposed to your strengths? It may be time to step up. Strategic marketing consultant Larry Bodine advises lawyers to look for "dormant" firm clients—those who are active, but underdeveloped in terms of engagement. If your firm has an existing relationship with a company, it's easier to offer additional services than it is to start from scratch with a cold contact. Look for opportunities to add value and deepen those relationships.

If you have a firm client that is a steady, but not spectacular, account, lavish some attention on the decision-makers to see if the relationship can be made more profitable. A firm can maximize marketing dollars by identifying needs among existing clients and offering firm lawyers who can provide the experience necessary to meet that need. Take someone from that small client or company to lunch or dinner and send them a copy of the latest breakthrough case that affects that company's docket. Treat the little client with the same level of love and attention that others give to the firm's larger clients. Remember: big oaks from little acorns grow. Plant seeds. Start watering the acorns in your business backyard.

Now let's talk about internal marketing—within your own firm or network.

Your colleagues should know what you do, what you're great at, and what kinds of matters you're looking for. If they don't, you're leaving opportunities on the table.

In evaluating your marketing ability, you should give a cold, analytical look at how you are perceived by your internal colleagues, since they can be a source of additional work and assignments to you. Are you viewed as the "go to" person in a particular area? Are you like my former-associate A, who had the quickest research fingers in the firm when it came to finding hard-to-locate law? Are you like Z, who could organize and report on any set of materials, no matter how complicated, in an almost supernaturally-short period of time? Are you the lawyer who will sleep at the office if necessary, to get something done on time? Or, are you the mystery lawyer who no one knows? Worse yet, are you the person no one wants to ask for help, because you will either say "no" or only provide a 50-percent effort?

If you aren't known as a go-to person in your firm, you have work to do.

Start with visibility. Invite a colleague you don't know well to coffee. Volunteer for an internal initiative. Join a pitch team. Even casual conversations at firm events can yield long-term opportunities.

Clients often do not know what other services a firm can offer;

it's also true that other lawyers within a firm often do not know the expertise of their colleagues. You may have a vague idea of the practice area of the lawyer down the hall, but they probably have the same limited understanding of your practice and background. Given the increased mobility of lawyers, you should assume that not everyone you work with knows about your prior legal experience.

Spend time with the lawyers in your firm, particularly if you are a lateral hire or otherwise new to the group. Make sure that all the people with whom you practice know your abilities and experiences. Think of how you want your peers to view you, and set about letting them know what your strengths are. Conversely, make sure you are familiar with the practice areas and talents of your colleagues. There may be other lawyers in the firm who have work in an area you are interested in. Consider how to persuade those lawyers to include you in their work or marketing efforts. Partners typically view business development as a team effort. Seize an opportunity to participate in one of the team presentations. Increase your internal visibility and recognition from firm members who may not know you. Your firm is your professional home, so get to know your professional siblings.

I once worked with a firm that created a trivia game for a retreat. Each question involved something about a lawyer's past cases or expertise. It was fun—and remarkably effective. Suddenly, people were learning about each other's skills without ever reading a bio.

You don't need a retreat to do that. A short conversation in the hallway or a five-minute chat before a Zoom call can build bridges. People refer work to those they know—and trust. Make sure you're someone they know. Another way to become acquainted with your coworkers' expertise is simply to ask each other about yourselves. It sounds quaint these days, but take some time to go to lunch with a lawyer in the firm with whom you do not typically work or socialize. Consider adding someone new to your afternoon Starbucks run. Everyone benefits when everyone participates. Most importantly, you and your firm will benefit when your team knows your abilities.

And finally, remember this: your firm is your professional home. Get to know your professional family. When you're top of mind internally, it becomes easier for others to send work your way.

KEYWORDS:

Colleagues, Extrovert

ADDITIONAL READING:

"Four Solid Strategies for Expanding Your Professional Network", Business News Daily Editor, Expert, February 10, 2020

"Networking in 2025: Strategies for Legal Professionals", https://www.jmc-legal.com/resources/blog/networking-in-2025--strategies-for-legal-professionals/

Contacts Analysis Worksheet

List the major professional activities you attended during the past 12 months. For each activity, list the following:

1. The new people you met at each event.
2. The personal details you learned from meeting them.
3. The business development results that occurred (e.g., got a significant new introduction, got an opportunity to make a presentation, got a good lead, nothing came of it).

Event	Contact	Info Learned	Results

Additional follow-up to be done:

_____

_____

_____

_____

_____

_____

PART III

MIND YOUR NETWORK

"Take care of your network, and your network will take care of you."

- Eden Abrahams

CHAPTER 7

DETERMINE YOUR MARKETING STRENGTHS

Now that you've been recognized as an expert and established your brand, your next step is to convert that cache on your desk into work. There are a variety of ways to do that. You need to identify the approach that best suits your personality and your targeted practice area. What works to woo patent law clients may not work to attract bankruptcy clients. You need to consider your area of practice, as well as your own personality.

Put another way: You've clarified your vision. You've honed your expertise. You've expanded your circle. Now it's time to ask: What kind of marketer are you?

The legal profession recognizes areas of expertise, but we lawyers seem to believe that every person with a law license should have an identical approach to the expert topic of business development. If you practice in an area geared to individual clients, why force yourself to attend corporate counsel meetings with corporations for which you offer no service? You wouldn't dream of accepting a case assignment totally out of your area of legal expertise, so why take on a marketing assignment that is totally out of your area of personal expertise? Successful marketing requires the same type of structured analytical approach that you are accustomed to using in your legal practice. Those skills just feel different to us when applied in the business development context. Learn to evaluate potential marketing events to identify those that best fit your marketing persona.

In other words, no two lawyers approach business development the same way, nor should they. The most effective rainmakers aren't clones—they're aligned with their strengths.

Start by being honest with yourself. Some lawyers thrive at networking events. Others would rather write articles, deliver presentations, or cultivate relationships one-on-one over coffee. Business development is not a "one size fits all" activity. It's a professional discipline that should be customized to your personality, your skills, and your practice area.

If your firm offers personality testing through HR or a business development department, take advantage of it. Insights from tools like StrengthsFinder, DISC, or even Myers-Briggs can illuminate what environments energize you—and what drains you.

If you're an extrovert, use that to your advantage. If you're an introvert, use that to your advantage. If you're a transactional lawyer who gets hives at the thought of speaking to a crowd, why sign up to give speeches at ABA seminars? On the other hand, if you're a ham who loves the prospect of a captive audience, and cannot remember what the Blue Book refers to, why devote countless painful hours to writing a scholarly article for a law journal? In other words, if writing is not your strong point, speak. If speaking is not your strongpoint, write. If you can do both, multi-task.

If you love public speaking but hate writing, pitch a CLE. If you're a strong writer but freeze up in front of an audience, build a blog or contribute to publications in your field. If you enjoy deep conversations with people, focus on one-on-one networking and referral-building. Don't force yourself into a mold that doesn't fit.

And while we're at it—don't chase the wrong audience. If your practice centers around estate planning for families, you probably don't need to attend corporate counsel panels. Choose venues and communities that align with your services and where potential clients and referrers already gather.

As an example, for a long time, I attended the ABA Convention every other year. As all lawyers know, that convention attracts thousands of practicing lawyers and corporate legal consumers, a.k.a. potential clients. Back in the days when the conference agenda came in hard-copy form, I would take the phone book-sized agenda and identify the presentations being done by lawyers I knew, or wanted to know. I planned to attend the presentations that included panel discussions by client representatives of companies I wanted to have on my personal client roster. I made advance calls to the lawyers I knew in the convention city and asked if I could attend any parties they were having. Once I got to the convention, I intentionally set about meeting the in-house lawyers and outside national counsel who assigned the type of work I wanted to do. In all the times I attended the ABA Convention, although I rarely knew anyone in advance, I made at least one connection that ultimately resulted in a work assignment.

I was able to do that because I'm an extrovert who relishes large crowds and new acquaintances. I had colleagues who had vastly different experiences in attending that convention, because they were overwhelmed by the crowds of strangers, and the lack of pre-existing connections. Their experience and mine were different, because of our personality differences and our marketing strengths. They were much more comfortable and effective in smaller, more structured environments.

For some, those big events can be overwhelming—and that's okay. Smaller bar committees, alumni gatherings, and focused roundtables might be a better fit. Your business development strategy should energize you, not exhaust you. Otherwise, you won't sustain it—and sustainability is key.

You just need to identify that unique aspect of your own personality that can be used to develop business and clients. Choose those venues and locations that work best for you. Play to your strengths. You will be happier with the process, and your results will be more fruitful..

KEYWORDS:

Insight, Honesty

ADDITIONAL READING:

"Best Tests to Help You Understand Your Strengths and Weaknesses" Forbes Coaches Council 2018, https://www.forbes.com/sites/ forbescoachescouncil/2018/01/22/best-tests-to-help-you-understand your-strengths-and-weaknesses/#18d-fe5cf495a

Marketing Personality Evaluation

1. Which parts of business development energize you?

_____

_____

_____

2. Which parts of business development do you find draining?

_____

_____

_____

3. What have people told you is your best business development skill?

_____

_____

_____

4. In business development, what comes easy for you that others find more difficult?

_____

_____

_____

5. In business development, what do you find difficult that may be easier for others?

_____

_____

_____

Summary: What do you think you do best when it comes to business development?

_____

_____

_____

CHAPTER 8

MAXIMIZE YOUR MARKETING

Time is money. Time is also a luxury. Time spent on business development is time you are not spending on your existing assignments or with your family and friends. Consequently, you want to be as efficient as possible when you devote time and money to business development activities. Make sure you keep track of the return—both in assignments and billings—from the marketing you do. What worked? What did not? One of my former colleagues was famous for saying "I love holding babies, but they can't send me work."

Determine how best to manage your very crowded calendar to accomplish goals that benefit you, as a lawyer, and the firm, as a business. Every hour you spend on business development is an hour you're not billing, prepping for trial, or spending with family. That means your marketing efforts need to be efficient, intentional, and results-driven.

Start with this question: *What's working?*

Too often, lawyers throw themselves into activities—joining boards, attending mixers, sponsoring tables—without stopping to measure the return. Some activities feed your soul, others your résumé, but only a few will feed your practice. Your goal is to identify those few.

The goal of a marketing program is not to meet every human on the face of the planet. The goal is to develop quality relationships that can be sustained over significant periods of time. People who don't hear from you are not likely to remember you have the exact expertise needed during their time of crisis. To put it another way; if you're out of sight, you're out of mind. Developing and maintaining human relationships makes your life more pleasant both at work and at home.

Keep your friends and existing clients in mind when you sketch out your list of potential business contacts. Those naturally ongoing relationships constitute some of your easiest sources of business. In the haste to become a marketing guru, "don't forget who brung you"—as we say in my home state of Texas.

Marketing research indicates that most lawyers and law firms receive the largest amount of their work from existing client contacts, whether those are current clients, or personnel from previous clients who have moved on to new jobs. Devote the sort of attention to maintaining business relationships that you devote to keeping up with social friends. Or, if you don't devote time to social friends, try to improve your social network while also focusing on the development of your business network. You need that balance.

Keep a record of where your work is coming from. Which relationships led to referrals? Which events actually produced introductions that turned into clients? Which publications generated inbound inquiries or speaking invitations? It's not enough to stay busy—you need to stay strategic.

Join legal, professional, and community organizations that afford you a chance to meet potential clients and referral sources. Evaluate them before signing up. Grade them once you've become involved. For example, assume you've paid for a membership in a professional organization that advertises itself as a good forum for meeting new clients. The cost of that membership should go into your marketing budget, and you should carefully document the number of calls, introductions, and referrals you get from either the organization or the people you meet through its activities. At the end of the year, if you've not generated any business from your membership, ask yourself whether you get enough non-business value from the organization to justify the cost, or whether you should spend that amount of your budget on something else. In other words, if it doesn't make a passing grade, move on.

Let's be clear: some non-revenue activities are still worth doing. Maybe you sit on a nonprofit board that aligns with your values. Maybe you mentor law students. Those are important contributions. But when it comes to business development, track what actually converts. Measure your time the way you measure billables: with intention.

Here are some metrics to use to evaluate those activities:

- What's the cost? (Time, money, energy)
- What's the outcome? (New business, increased visibility, stronger relationships)
- Is it repeatable? (Can this be part of a sustainable strategy?)

Not every worthy activity will end up being productive, despite your efforts. Early in my career, I joined a strategic planning group thinking it would lead to referrals. I was welcomed with open arms, gained practical insights, and expanded my business knowledge. However, not a single client came from it. Later, I shifted to a different business association more aligned with the legal services I offered. My business development goals were better served by participating in a different business group, which ultimately turned out to be a better source of referrals and introductions for me.

Lesson learned: don't confuse activity with progress. In other words, remember to distinguish activity from outcome.

Also, don't overlook internal referrals. If you're at a firm, consider this: are your colleagues aware of all the services you can offer their clients? When someone in your firm refers you a matter, be sure to show your appreciation—and be prepared to return the favor. A good internal network can lead to steady streams of work.

Likewise, if a client comes to you with a matter outside your expertise, introduce them to someone who can handle it well.

That helps the client, strengthens your reputation, and builds professional goodwill.

If you're in a firm, don't overlook the value of internal cross-marketing. The next time an existing client needs legal assistance in an area outside your expertise, canvas your practice group to see if there's someone among you who can handle the problem. One-stop shopping is convenient for all of us, including our clients. If you can get the work in the door, make sure you get financial credit for the relationship, whether that's billing credit, managing credit, or some other type of financial recognition. On the other hand, if your firm cannot provide the necessary expertise, assist the client in finding a lawyer who is competent to handle the problem. You'll have made a friend on both sides of the transaction and will be in a position to receive another call from the client when the issue is within your wheelhouse. You'll also have a potential reciprocal referral—when the other lawyer faces a legal conundrum that is better-suited to your expertise than theirs.

Managing Partner Forum President John Remsen reminds his seminar attendees that you must be consistent in your marketing efforts. A start-and-stop approach to business development undermines your overall success. You need to schedule business development tasks and make them part of your daily routine. Not every activity has to be lengthy or time-consuming. You can send an email to a contact about an issue you know they're following. You can send a text to an existing client about a court case they might find interesting. Get into the habit of sending something out on Monday, because that gives you the rest of the week to follow up and move forward on your project.

Above all, be persistent. Business development isn't a seasonal activity—it's a career habit. Don't disappear for six months and then wonder why the phone isn't ringing. Even a small action, repeated regularly, builds momentum. Send an article to a contact. Share a court ruling with a client. Follow up on a connection you made at a conference.

Here's a tip: send one outreach email every Monday morning.

Start your week with a point of connection. It's a small act—but it compounds over time.

And while you're at it, evaluate your efforts twice a year. Use the end of June and the end of December to conduct a personal audit of your business development efforts: what worked, what didn't, and where your time is best spent moving forward. Those activities that don't further your book of business may be perfectly legitimate underakings—like holding those babies—but they may not be actual business development. Identify those activities that are likely to get work for you. Emphasize those rather than attending the purely social activities in the profession that may be fun but don't help you fulfill your goal of getting business.

Set some concrete goals, so you can determine the progress you've made. Become adept at using the task list and calendaring functions of whatever software program you use, then put the specific tasks on your list into the program, and set it to send you reminders. For example, if your goal is to gain one new client a year, write that down, and work to accomplish it. If your goals are more ambitious than that, determine what you need to do to balance the time requirement of developing those clients and providing them the level of service that keeps them in the fold—and their receivables in your column of the ledger.

Marketing doesn't have to be overwhelming. It just has to be deliberate.

KEY TERMS:

Economical, Meticulous

ADDITIONAL READING:

"How to Maximize Your Content Marketing Budget", Victor Smushkevich, Forbes Councils Member, Forbes Agency Council 2020

The Ultimate Guide to Content Marketing for Law Firms in 2025,by Laurie Villanueva, March 6th, 2025 • Content Marketing | Blog, https://good2bsocial.com/the-ultimate-guide-to-content-marketing-for-law-firms-in-2025/

Marketing Activities Analysis

Time devoted to marketing in the past 12 months: _____ (hours)

List the major marketing activities in which you were involved during the past 12 months.

For each activity, list the following:

1. The amount of time it took (e.g. hours, days)
2. Your comfort level in doing it (e.g. high, medium, low)
3. The results that occurred (e.g. got significant new business, got an opportunity to make a presentation, got a good lead, nothing came of it)

Activity	Time	Comfort Level	Results

Key Learnings:

_____
_____
_____
_____

CHAPTER 9

MAKE A CONNECTION

Clients hire lawyers, not just law firms. The name of the firm may get you the interview; however, getting hired for a client assignment resembles every other job interview you've ever had. The interviewer wants to know the qualifications of the applicant. Do they have the right experience? Do they have the right professional contacts? Do they have a price structure that meets the client's budget? And, what do their references and co-counsel say about them?

Each hiring decision includes a subjective component. In other words, in-house counsel deciding between comparably-qualified candidates consider personal characteristics along with the objective data. They need to hire the right lawyer for the job. There may be some high profile, bet-the-company matters where the Board of Directors chooses the firm with the right pedigree, rather than the right lawyer—but for the majority of cases and assignments, the firm name is not the deciding factor. The right person is the deciding factor.

Every client interaction is, at its core, a relationship. When a potential client chooses a lawyer, they're not just evaluating credentials. They're asking themselves:

- Does this lawyer understand my business?
- Will they be responsive?
- Are they practical? Strategic? Efficient?
- Can I trust them?

Often, the deciding factor has nothing to do with résumé bullet points. It comes down to personal connection. When clients are choosing among capable professionals, they default to the person they believe will be easiest to work with and most aligned with their needs.

I once heard a general counsel explain her strategy at industry events. She made a point to observe how lawyers behaved outside the pitch room—in casual settings, at dinners, even in line at the coffee cart. She wanted to see what kind of people they are when they're not in client-solicitation mode. She watched how they treated wait staff. "If you're rude to the server," she said, "you're probably rude to my staff. And I won't hire you." She limits, or eliminates, the use of lawyers who "misbehave" in those casual settings.

What a great point, and one that we sometimes overlook. We all—myself included—spend so much time focused on our professional qualifications, we sometimes forget we're all in the people business. Personality and character are just as important to many clients as the robust curriculum vitae.

Her story stuck with me. It was a reminder that people notice far more than our polished bios and practice group highlights. They pay attention to character. Respect. Professionalism. All the things that make a working relationship productive.

If you're not nice to the waiter, the client can make the reasonable assumption you'll not be nice to her secretary. There may be some lawyers who can get, and keep, clients without observing any social niceties, but you wouldn't be reading this book if you had so many clients, and such a large accounts receivable, that you could ignore the human element of business development. The biblical admonition to do unto others as you would have them do unto you applies as well to the legal world as it does to the real world.

Treating people well extends to co-counsel and opposing counsel, too. During my career, as much of my work has come through the recommendations and referrals of other lawyers, including opposing counsel, as it has from my concerted business development efforts. Don't underestimate your network of colleagues. Friends and colleagues know your abilities and can recount those strengths to their clients, who may need additional legal help. Also, don't discount your adversaries. Opposing counsel, oddly enough, often have the ability to make suggestions about candidates for legal assignments. They recognize a tough, yet ethical, opponent. I've received referrals from adversaries who respected my ethics, preparation, and courtroom demeanor. Those connections matter for you, too. They see how you work under pressure, and their recommendation carries weight. In other words, be professional—even with your opponents. Your stress level will be lower, and your network will be bigger. Creeps have short lifespans in big business, despite the common belief that good guys finish last.

So how do you build meaningful connections? It starts with presence. When you meet someone—at a conference, on a call, or over coffee—treat that moment as the beginning of a relationship, not a transaction. Ask thoughtful questions. Listen. Follow up.

Track where your matters come from. Who referred you? Who introduced you to your last three clients? Who have you referred cases to recently—and why? If you don't know, start keeping a log. This helps you recognize patterns and reciprocate value, where there is an opportunity to do so. Finally, be generous with your professionalism. When you send work to another lawyer—whether because of conflict, specialization, or bandwidth—choose someone you trust. And if you consistently refer out but never receive anything in return, it may be time to reevaluate those relationships. Business development, like any partnership, should be mutually beneficial.[2]

2 There are legal and ethical rules applicable to legal referrals. Additionally, some firms have guidelines and procedures applicable to case and client referrals. Be sure you understand both the ethical rules and any applicable firm procedures before you refer a case to another lawyer. A discussion of those legal issues is beyond the scope of this guide; however, you should be familiar with them and adhere to them as part of your own ethical practice.

The connections you make with your clients, your colleagues, and opposing lawyers all contribute to the development of your business network. Devote time and attention to the social factors of those connections. No marketing plan will be successful unless you do.

KEYWORDS:

Friendship, Civility

ADDITIONAL READING:

How to Win Friends and Influence People, Dale Carnegie; "What Dale Carnegie's How to Win Friends and Influence People Can Teach the Modern Worker", Jessica Weisberg, The New Yorker, April 2, 2018

Work Source Analysis

From where did your last three case assignments originate?[3]

1. _____

2. _____

3. _____

When, if ever, did you receive a case referral?

_____

From whom did you last receive a case referral?

_____

To whom did you send your last three case referrals?

1. _____

2. _____

3. _____

For each referral you made, why did you refer the matter to that particular lawyer or firm?

_____

_____

---

3 *In-firm assignments and referrals count for tracking purposes. Give the same attention to your firm partners and professional colleagues who send you work as you do to those external colleagues who send you work. Also, see footnotes 1 and 2 above, regarding ethical considerations for referrals.*

PART IV

CONVERT CONTACTS INTO CLIENTS

"Every great business is built on friendship."

~ J.C. Penney

CHAPTER 10

TRACK YOUR CONNECTIONS

You've made connections. Now the real work begins. Stay in touch. Converting a connection into a business source happens because you have established a relationship. Meeting is not enough on its own. The business collaboration happens because you created a lasting connection. Fleeting meetings result in lasting connections in Hollywood, not in the legal world.

Sustaining those connections—*and strategically cultivating them*—is what transforms contacts into clients. That requires consistent, intentional follow-up.

You must nourish the network you've established. Social media facilitates keeping your name in front of your connections. That media presence takes work. You need to have a schedule for preparing and sharing useful, substantive content. You should have an extensive email database you can use to provide relevant information and updates to your clients, your colleagues, your referral sources, your friends, and your family. Out of sight, out of mind—not where you want to be after having done all the work to develop the network.

A "happy birthday" email—sent to someone you know well enough to send such a thing—means much more than a generic holiday card at the end of the year. It's also significantly cheaper for your marketing budget. Likewise, sending a handwritten note, with a copy of an interesting bar journal article, doesn't cost much, yet might be appreciated by an overworked in-house lawyer who does not have enough time or budget to attend a costly CLE seminar on the topic.

Too many lawyers let promising introductions fade. A great conversation at a conference goes nowhere. A referral partner drifts into the background. An article is published and never shared. Why? Because we get busy. And business development moves down the priority list when client work and firm deadlines start to stack up.

But here's the truth: out of sight is out of mind. And in business development, invisibility is the enemy of opportunity.

That's why you need a system to track your outreach. Whether it's a spreadsheet, a CRM tool, or even a dedicated notebook, create a place to record:

- Who you've met
- Where you met them
- What you talked about
- What follow-up is needed
- When to reach out next

Even something as simple as "Sent article on new legislation—follow up in 30 days" can make the difference between a missed chance and a new engagement.

Use technology to your advantage. Create calendar reminders. Automate check-ins. Use contact management apps. If you're using Linkedin or email newsletters to share your insights, track who's engaging. If you send a holiday card, make a note of who responds. Small touchpoints create familiarity—and familiarity builds trust.

And don't forget your digital presence. When was the last time you updated your website biography? Added a new speaking engagement? Linked to your latest publication? Remember to update your website information frequently. Your website biography should not be like your high school yearbook: carved in stone with an out-of-date photograph and dated haircut. Corporate clients often find information about counsel in the same way the rest of the world does—they do an Internet search for your website and read your biography. Your biography should be a living, breathing document that is updated as information changes—including any stylish new haircuts.

If you write, be sure to send the link to your latest article to those clients and colleagues who may benefit from the information. Make sure you link your publications to the website or online biography, so anyone seeking information on you and your firm will have easy access to your library of writings.

If you speak, be sure to let your clients and colleagues know about events in advance, so they have the chance to attend if they want. Bar organizations and community organizations often need speakers for conferences, lunches, or other events. Make sure the audience is one that is logical for your business model, and for the types of clients you want to recruit for your portfolio. For example, if you provide specialty intellectual property services for small businesses, a local chamber of commerce group might constitute an appropriate audience; whereas, a group of healthcare workers might not. Try to develop speaking materials that can be used more than once, so you can present on short notice. Your visual aids and handouts should include your name, your firm name, your logo, and your preferred contact method—phone or email. Include a QR code to simplify their search for you. As Patrick Fuller at ALM Marketing is famous for saying, "It isn't who you know that counts; it's who knows you." You want to increase both the number you know and the number who know you.

Marketing is like real estate: location, location, location. Once you make that contact, you must follow up. Research indicates that most people never follow-up. A few will make a second follow-up. Almost none make a third follow-up. Pitifully, few make a fourth follow-up.

And here's a powerful truth from the world of sales: it takes multiple interactions before someone engages your services. Studies suggest most people need at least seven meaningful "touches" before making a buying decision. In legal terms, that means seven moments of recognition: an article, a follow-up email, a lunch, a panel discussion, a Linkedin message, a referral, a news mention.

Those figures are consistent with the data from non-legal sales research, which show the following:

- Only three percent of sales are made after first contact.
- An average of seven contacts before a sale is made (18 months to close deal).
- 80 percent of all sales are made after five contacts.
- 87 percent of people who request information will eventually buy.
- 48 percent of people give up after one contact.
- 25 percent more give up after two contacts.
- 12 percent more give up after three contacts.
- 5 percent more give up after four contacts.
- 90 percent never get followed-up with more than four times.

Most lawyers give up after one or two attempts. But the persistent, professional, helpful ones—the ones who show up over time—are the ones who win the business.

So be strategic. Stay visible. Follow up. And repeat. Why is that important? Because marketing gurus, rather than the above-mentioned studies, say it takes at least eight touchpoints—legitimate contacts—with a target to convert them into a client. Whether it takes seven, or eight, or some larger number of connections, if you continue to follow up, you'll be among the minority of lawyers developing an ongoing relationship with a potential client.

You should be spending lunch opportunities with people you know—like the people you went to law school with, the people you went to college with who are in business and leading productive lives, clients, former clients, and co-workers. Those are the people who are most likely to send you business, because you understand what they need, and they understand what you have to offer.

On the other hand, don't be a stalker. Contacts and interactions need to be logical and add value to the recipient. The people whose work you are seeking have busy lives and demanding schedules. Just following up to follow up will not advance your cause. You don't want to be the lawyer whose name elicits groans from in-house counsel when you pop up in an email, or when your voice comes through the telephone.

One of the most aggressive business developers I ever encountered had a full-time assistant who called companies, clients, and other lawyers on her behalf. Their marketing budget must have been staggering, because each week brought a new hard-copy, snail-mail letter, invariably followed in a day, or two, by a call from the assistant, advising that she had scheduled a lunch meeting for me with her boss on a certain date at a local restaurant and wanting my confirmation I would be there.

There was no advance call to my assistant to find out if I was interested, available, or hungry on the appointed date. There was no intermediate question of whether her lunch plans were consistent with my calendar. After doing some discrete inquiries, I found that every person that lawyer met, whether at court, a seminar, the movies, or the grocery store, was besieged in the same way.

I never learned whether she actually generated any work from the full-court press, but I finally fell off the distribution list for her mailings and call list.

I do know I never joined her for lunch.

You should not use her approach as your model. You want to be persistent, but you don't want to be the marketing pariah. Be useful. Be patient. And, be in touch.

KEYWORDS:

Self-Awareness, Balance

ADDITIONAL READING:

"Everything You Need to Know About Touchpoints in Marketing" https://blog.tangiblewords.com/everything-you-need-to-know-about touchpoints-in-marketing-1

Business Development Schedule

What are the three most important insights you gained from this chapter?

1. _____

2. _____

3. _____

Within the next seven days, what three things will you do to follow up on business connections you've made?

1. _____

2. _____

3. _____

Within the next 30 days, what three things will you do to expand your business development network?

1. _____

2. _____

3. _____

Within the next 60 days, what three things will you do to further your business development goals?

1. _____

2. _____

3. _____

CHAPTER 11

ASK FOR THE WORK

You don't get what you don't ask for, and you have to ask for the work. No matter how impressive you are, how many people know you, or how many people you know, all your business development efforts are for naught if you don't get work on your desk and dollars in your column of accounts receivables at the end of the year.

Clients are not mind readers. You cannot expect a busy in-house lawyer to intuitively know you want to do more work for her or him. However, that same marketing research we saw in the previous chapter, which explains the number of touchpoints required to develop a relationship, also reveals that very few lawyers are willing to ask for the assignment once they establish the relationship.

Here's the simple truth: if you want to develop your own book of business, you have to learn how to ask for the work.

This is the part where many lawyers get stuck. They do everything right—build expertise, cultivate relationships, attend events, write articles, give speeches—and then stop short of the actual ask. But no amount of visibility replaces the clarity of a direct request.

Asking for the work isn't pushy. It's professional. It's also crucial to the development of your own power within the firm's financial structure.

I did a presentation for a women's Lawyer group some years ago and discussed the necessity of asking for the business.

Afterwards, one of the audience members approached me for advice on how to convert a client relationship into actual assignments. She explained to me that she had done an assignment for a client who really seemed to like her work.

She said, "I keep hinting that I would like to do more work, but he never sends any."

I asked her if she had ever said the words "I would like to do more work for you."

"No," she said. "That would be too forward. What do you think I should do?"

"You should be that forward," I replied.

As I explained to her, clients are like everyone else. They're busy. They don't have time to guess what you want. Business people assume that lawyers will display the same level of articulate advocacy in obtaining business they apply to handling the legal assignments they have been hired to take. In other words, they want a clear explanation of what it is that you're seeking. It is okay to say, "I enjoyed working with you on this project and would like to be considered the next time you need legal help. What do I need to do to be considered for additional assignments?"

You're not going to get power within the profession, nor in your law firm, if you cannot articulate what you want. You have spent time, money, and effort developing a relationship that can lead to more work—ask for that work and remember to ask for credit for it once the work arrives at the firm.

Make sure you understand how origination and credit are handled once you receive the work. Know the difference between being a working attorney and being a relationship partner. Learn how your firm allocates credit for introductions, billing, supervising, and managing. Then make your efforts visible. And be sure to ask your firm for the financial credit for whatever level of relationship you have to the work you bring in.

Your firm likely uses some form of "assignment origination analysis," even if it's informal. Track your contributions and learn how they influence your compensation. These aren't just internal politics—they're mechanisms of professional leverage. That leverage is the power you're building with the expansion of your client portfolio.

If your firm doesn't have a clear process, start by documenting your own contributions. Keep track of the clients you bring in, the matters you lead, and the relationships you help grow. Even in informal systems, reputations are built on patterns—and patterns start with data. Keep that in mind as you look for opportunities to expand your personal book of business.

You also must develop the ability to ask again if you don't get the business the first time. Even if you're the perfect candidate for a specific assignment, there could be a hundred corporate considerations that have nothing to do with you but result in you not receiving the assignment. Rejection may be impersonal. You'll be disappointed, and rightly so, but you should not be paralyzed. "No" on a particular assignment does not necessarily mean "never." Many lawyers view business development rejections as permanent. You should view them as "no, for now"—just like the denial of a non-dispositive motion in a case you're handling.

If you are the appropriate choice for a matter you did not receive, be gracious and adhere to your plan. Your time will come. Ask again.

KEYWORDS:

Patience, Tenacity

ADDITIONAL READING:

"How Do I Ask for Business?" Ask the Experts, Legal Marketing Association, 2013, https://www.attorneyatwork.com/how-do-i-ask-for-business/

Assignment Origination Analysis

List the five largest matters you brought in/worked on during the past 12 months

Matter	Source	Marketing Activity Involved

1. Draft Three Professional Asks for additional work:

(Examples: "If an opportunity arises, I'd love to be considered for X," or "I would like to be on the pitch team for Acme Company work.")

○ _____

○ _____

○ _____

2. Identify Three Prospective Clients or Contacts to follow up with for more work:

○ _____

○ _____

○ _____

3. Next Step Identify a client or contact from whom to request a new assignment in the next month

_____

_____

CHAPTER 12

MANAGE THE RELATIONSHIP

Back in the 1980s—when teenagers bought posters—I owned a poster of Garfield, the cartoon cat, with the caption: "It's not the having, it's the getting that counts." It hung on the door of my tiny, little closet in my tiny, little dormitory room. I thought it was a cute explanation of the internal drive necessary for success—don't be satisfied with what you have. As I grew older, however, I realized that the sentiment was quite different, and the moral of that poster no longer fit my approach to success. Whichever of my interpretations is correct, we can all agree that the sentiment is the opposite of the goal of business development.

Expanding your client portfolio means that you must value both the "getting" and the "having" of the business. Your financial portfolio, and your resulting role within your firm, depend on both halves of that equation. If you're going to be the top biller/originator/rainmaker in your firm, you have to develop clients and keep them. You need continuity to solidify your piece of the compensation pie.

Like all human relationships, the attorney-client relationship requires your time and attention. After you've invested the time and emotional energy to implement a plan, established your brand within the profession, networked unceasingly, and converted contacts into clients, the last thing you want to do is lose that relationship to another lawyer or law firm.

The care and feeding of clients requires thought and persistence. The protocol you used to get the work will help you establish a process of winning a new client, but that's only the beginning.

The real value—the long-term opportunity—comes from managing the relationship with care, attention, and consistency.

Great client service doesn't just mean being responsive or turning in high-quality work, although you have to provide both of those things. It means becoming a trusted advisor. It means anticipating needs, communicating effectively, and helping your client succeed beyond the four corners of the legal file.

That's how you go from outside counsel to indispensable partner.

Start by reviewing any billing guidelines the client has, and make sure you adhere to them. Ask about the client's preferred method of communication. Some like phone calls. Some like emails. Some like weekly reports, some monthly, some quarterly, and some no reports at all. You cannot guess what the client will want. Just like getting the business in the first place, you must ask what they want regarding logistics of handling the business aspects of the engagement.

Ensure that bills are correct and go out in a timely fashion. Make sure that the invoices conform to the client's preferred format. Invoices serve both to generate a payment for your work and to inform the client of the activities you've performed on their behalf. Treat them like any other written work product. They are a reflection of you and your firm, so ensure that someone with a good eye has proofread the text, and that the text communicates the firm's work. In-house lawyers have to review outside-counsel bills. Be sure to minimize the drudgery associated with that task on your client's desk. You should bear the burden of the first review. If the entries don't make sense to you, they not only will not make sense to your client, but they may also result in a delay in payment, which undercuts your goal of maximizing your financial footprint within your firm.

If Widget Company of America's billing guidelines declare the company does not pay for a certain cost, ensure that the invoice does not contain a charge for that cost. Or better yet, show the cost and zero it out, so the client is aware the cost has been incurred, but knows they are not paying for it. Instead, demonstrate that the expense has been written-off or absorbed by the firm. Prepare budgets for your engagements and discuss them with your in-house counterpart. Consider that part of the strategy of the case and your client development. Clients have budgets. Be sure you understand what they can afford to spend on a worthy dispute, so you can provide them with both legal strategy and business options relating to the cost.. Lawyers cost money. From a balance-sheet perspective, legal costs are expenses—not assets. No matter how valuable your legal work for a client may be, the stockholders, accountants, and auditors simply view you as a cost. Justify that cost by providing the best business case for the strategy being employed. How do you do that?

One of my colleagues, I will call him Bob, sends each of his clients a letter at the end of each month, detailing the firm's accomplishments on the client's behalf during the previous month. He justifies the cost of his services by highlighting how those services provide value to the organization. The letter is a freebie. He does not bill for preparing it. However, the correspondence recounts the hearings, motions, depositions, settlements, and other activities the firm has undertaken on behalf of the client that month. That detailed list of activities illustrates the extent of the efforts his team made to defend the company's positions and demonstrates the importance of having his team members as its advocates.

In theory, his firm's monthly billing invoice provides the same information as the monthly marketing letter, but his concise summary gives a more readable version of the information in a format that can more easily be absorbed by the recipient. It can also be easily forwarded and shared with others in the organization, multiplying Bob's name recognition within the client's organization. At the end of the year, Bob can refer to those letters as a convenient resource for explaining not only why it's appropriate for the client to continue the relationship, but also why the company should consider his request for a rate increase. He maintains his relationships because he manages the communication with the client. He gets paid because the client knows the value of the work being done.

The letters serve an additional, internal purpose, too. Bob uses those same letters as part of his packet for the compensation committee at the end of the year to illustrate his value to the firm's overall book of business. While his originations and working-attorney statistics reflect the monetary value of his work, his newsletter-like presentation of the details gives life to the raw numbers and justifies his (large) yearly bonus.

You need to manage the financial relationship on both tracks: external, with the client, and internal, with management. Keep that second aspect in mind as you document the importance of your work during the year. Because the materials have been compiled as the year progresses, you'll already have them easily accessible when the time comes to negotiate an increase for yourself.

Another of my colleagues, I'll call her Betty, manages her relationships in a quite different, yet equally proactive, way. Betty provides a succinct summary of the client's strategic strengths at the beginning of each discussion, followed by an explanation of the associated risks and the prospects for minimizing or eliminating the risks. She voices the concerns that she knows the client has and provides tangible suggestions for controlling those aspects of the dispute or project that can reasonably be controlled. Betty follows each discussion with a short memo to the client which covers the highlights of the risk and reward considerations.

Her approach benefits from also giving the client the satisfaction of knowing that their legal dollars are being invested wisely. Previewing the issues ahead also previews the work necessary to minimize the risk of an unacceptable outcome. Like our male colleague, Betty keeps a stack of contemporaneous writings she compiles at the end of the year to remind her client of the value she and her team added to their portfolio during the year. She takes that same pile of materials, with a nice overview summary, to her firm's annual compensation committee meeting. The stack of paper is a visual reminder of her value to the law firm and ensures that the financial discussion reflects concrete benchmarks to maximize her bonus and annual draw.

You want to do something to legitimately keep your name and good work in front of the client, whether you use Bob's approach, or Betty's, or something entirely different. Use calendar reminders to remind you to send those summary letters. If you have a secretary or assistant, they can keep a running list of client activities for you, so you can easily convert it into a more formal communication at the end of the month. The end product requires a little of your time, but pays a lot of value.

Those letters also serve to keep your name in the forefront as the contact person, if you have people assisting you on your cases. Preparing a letter that goes over your signature communicates that you remain in charge of the work. Remember: you want to both get and have that client relationship long-term.

Also remember: you want to have that existing stash of explanatory documents to show the compensation committee at the end of the year. You've done the work. You should get the financial credit and the firm's acknowledgement of your valuable role in the organization. Sometimes, it's not the survival of the fittest that counts, it's the survival of the persistent and the visible. Show your partners your work, so they'll give you the Power at the Table you deserve.

Now, go get 'em.

KEYWORDS:

Commitment, Power

ADDITIONAL READING:

Shavon Jones, "How to Make It Rain and Slay the Game Today," Law Practice Today (American Bar Association), March 17, 2025

Relationship Management Schedule

Client Name	Notifica-tion Task (email, letter, spread-sheet)	Frequency (monthly, quarterly, annual)	Drafting Responsi-bility (you, associate, assistant)	Date Sent

EPILOGUE

EVEN COWGIRLS GET THE CLIENTS

I grew up on a cattle ranch in Frogville, in the Southeastern corner of Oklahoma. We were not a family of lawyers.

Growing up on that ranch, however, prepared me for the practice of law in unanticipated ways. I knew that the cows must be fed, whether you're making money or not. They must be fed no matter how bad the weather, or how tired you are. And, they must be treated and medicated—no matter how inconvenient or expensive. In other words, ranching is like practicing law and caring for one's clients and employees. Practicing law is that same sort of 24-hour-a-day labor of love and inconvenience. I thought, however, that getting away from the "natural fertilizer" and bales of hay was going to lead to a more genteel way of life.

As it turns out, there is nothing genteel about the practice of law. It has a rough and tumble nature to it that requires the individual lawyer to be both a counselor and an entrepreneur. I quickly discovered that neither living on the ranch nor attending law school had prepared me for the business of practicing law. Who knew that was going to be so difficult?

The answer, I suppose, is that probably everyone reading this, knew that. I, however, was a starry-eyed, young lawyer trying to navigate the legal world. I expected to go to my first job and stay there forever with the firm providing all the clients, work, and opportunities that I would need. That, of course, was not how things worked out.

In the early days of my practice, I spent a lot of time proving that I belonged—at the table, in the courtroom, on the call. I was younger than most, didn't come from a long line of lawyers, and didn't have a portfolio of clients to my name. What I had was work ethic, persistence, and a belief that if I showed up consistently and delivered real value, someone would notice.

Someone did.

Over time, opportunities came. Some were earned through effort, others through relationships, and a few through sheer luck. But the ones that mattered most—the ones that built a book of business and a career of influence—came from putting myself out there, over and over again.

Not by being loud. Not by being perfect. But by being present.

That's how it works. You don't have to be the most connected, the most extroverted, or the most experienced. You just have to be deliberate. Clear about your goals. Thoughtful about your value. Persistent in your efforts.

You have to show up when it matters—and sometimes when it seems like it doesn't.

You also have to be willing to take the reins. To build something of your own. That's what Power at the Table really means. It's not about bravado or dominance. It's about ownership. It's about having power within the profession and your firm because you brought something no one else did—your clients, your credibility, your voice.

Whether you're a partner, a new associate in a towering firm, or a solo practitioner serving your hometown, you have the ability to create that power. One relationship at a time. One matter at a time. One result at a time.

I've been in courtrooms and boardrooms. I've run boutique firms and led offices of national ones. I've seen how unpredictable the legal world can be—and how resilience, strategy, and a sense of humor can carry you through it.

And I've learned that the lawyers who build the strongest careers are the ones who stop waiting for someone to give them clients and control—and go get them for themselves.

So saddle up. This is your practice, your career, your legacy. No matter where you started, you have the power to shape where you're going.

Even cowgirls like myself—and cowboys, and counselors of every stripe—get the clients.

Final Takeaway:

Own your path. Build your client list. Claim your power.

ABOUT THE AUTHOR

Sharla Frost is an award-winning litigator, a bestselling author, and a champion for the next generation. Over her celebrated almost 40 year legal career, Sharla established herself as one of the nation's leading trial attorneys, overcoming obstacles and mentoring young attorneys. Her influential first book, Power At the Table, quickly became an Amazon bestseller, guiding women lawyers and entrepreneurs to build their own client base and take control of their career success.

In Power At The Table2, Sharla expands her target audience, sharing how her strategies for networking, cultivating relationships and marketing yourself are applicable, not only to attorneys, but to anyone who wants to maximize their professional opportunities.

Sharla's expertise goes beyond the courtroom. She is a sought-after speaker, sharing her wisdom on litigation, negotiation, communication, and leadership at law schools and professional associations nationwide.

Raised on a working cattle ranch in Frogville, Oklahoma, Sharla's childhood was filled with adventure and wonder that continues to inspire her. After retiring from the courtroom, she returned to her hometown where she invested her time and talent in her local community. She also began writing the beloved Frogville children's book series—stories that encourage courage, creativity, friendship, and the magic of possibility for readers of all ages. Her imaginative tales remind us that, no matter our differences, by working together, we can achieve the extraordinary.

www.ingramcontent.com/pod-product-compliance
Lightning Source LLC
Chambersburg PA
CBHW040908210326
41597CB00029B/5009